A Bible for My Pillow

Ms. Grace

THIS BOOK IS A FIRST DRAFT. IT CONTAINS
TYPOS AND ERRORS. THIS IS INTENTIONAL TO
SHOW THAT GOD USES THINGS THAT ARE NOT
PERFECT.

For Jesus Christ who walked before me, with me, and after me through hell and called to me through the darkness, even when I didn't call on Him. I am forever grateful to You.

For my daughters. I'd walk across the earth and back for you so you didn't have to. When you were born, I said I'd do anything for you. My love for you is infinite, and Jesus loves you even more than I do.

For my husband.

"I went through hell so you can put on this helmet."

-Steven Furtick

Acknowledgements

Thank you to God. You saved me, reached down into the depths of hell to pull me out, and brought me through difficult times to be alive and in the position to share my testimony.

Thanks to my family who helped me in the most difficult season of my life. The significance of your support, love, and care is immeasurable. I came to Michigan with almost nothing, and through love and kindness, me and my girls had more than we needed.

Thank you to my daughter who is tough as nails. You demonstrated unconditional love and modeled a giving heart that led me at times. My sweet girl, you are so special.

Thanks to Pastor Steven Furtick and Elevation Church. The sermons produced by you and your church kept me sane and moving forward in difficult times.

Thank you to Pastor Herb of The Grove church. I value your consistent support and influence.

Table of Contents

Introduction: Keep Your Friends Close but Your Enemies Closer

A dark figure with red eyes clung to my arm and looked up at me waiting to scare me as I locked eyes with it. Immediately, my heart fell into my chest, and what felt like a cold ice cube on my skin ran from the bottom of my arm up to the top of my shoulder and then to the back of my neck. My breath left me as pressure crushed my neck, and I gasped for air. I looked across the living room at my husband who had no idea what was happening. My vision started to close as oxygen continued to leave my brain, and desperate for any kind of relief, I jumped off the couch and ran out the front door into the open air under the moon where I finally breathed in a breath of fresh air like a person who was drowning and finally emerged from underwater.

Fast forward two years, and I laid in bed at night trying to fall asleep. As usual, I was tucked in with a tickle on my foot and a "Good night" that rang in my head. Without hesitation, a pair of hands stroked my cheek, climbed in bed next to me, and ran its fingers through my hair. Accustomed to its routine, I rolled my eyes in the dark and said out loud, "Leave me alone so I can sleep."

****

Keep your friends close but your enemies closer. I'd heard people say this before, but I never really understood what it meant until I lived with a demon.

In 2021, my family landed itself in an apartment in Beaufort, South Carolina that housed a demon. We intended on living in the apartment for a couple months until we were supposed to move on military orders. However, this didn't happen. Instead, we fulfilled an entire 12-month lease in the apartment, and during this time, we encountered a living hell that ended up destroying our lives.

If you've ever watched *The Conjuring* or *The Exorcist*, you'd understand what I mean when I say, our time in the apartment turned into a real-life and modern version of one of these movies. A dark figure walked the hall and around our bedrooms at night, doors slammed and shut by themselves, and what felt like a cold hand would touch and press against our skin. When we eventually left the apartment, we thought we left the demon behind. It turned out, it was just waiting. Waiting for an opportunity. A person. An encounter. A prey. A prey to trap in the devil's grip. A trap of torture, entanglement, confusion, frustration, manipulation, and abuse. I was unlucky enough to get caught in this trap. I begged God every day to get me out, but He had other plans for me.

This story is about an impossible situation that Jesus saved me from. It's about a walk through hell with a demon that intended to kill me but couldn't because of the hand of God. Looking back, it was a journey that involved so much pain and confusion that I often thought it would be better to be dead than alive. The journey itself was so daunting and traumatic that I am unable to tell you about it in full detail.

Things from this part of my life still taunt me at times. Seeing the time 8:00 p.m. on the clock still sends chills down my spine, and so does the sound of a metal doorstop whizzing back and forth and a door grinding on a frame that's too small when it's opened or closed. The smell of urine can send me straight into a pure mode of panic that will send me pacing around my house trying to catch my breath, the sight of a spider feels like someone punched me in the gut, and a shadow dancing across the wall sends a feeling of uneasiness from my throat all the way down into my stomach.

During the time I lived with the demon, I asked God why He would put me through such conditions almost daily, but now that He pulled me out of it and I can see it in reverse, I can confidently look back and say, I understand and that I'd have it no other way.

Not anticipating and ending that entailed me making it out of the situation alive and sane and in trying to kill me physically, mentally, and spiritually, the demon accidentally revealed itself from its disguise. If the devil could have his way now, I'd be dead, but I'm not because he quickly relearned what he already knows: he isn't in charge, and the Big Man upstairs is.

Now that I'm on the other side of my journey with the demon and made it out alive, I am living proof that Jesus is all powerful, and furthermore, I now know one of the devil's dirty little secrets that I fully intend on spreading like a wildfire: Schizophrenia isn't a mental health disorder; it's a demon possession.

Chapter 1: The First Encounter

When I first encountered the demon in our apartment in 2021, I awoke to it standing over me as I slept in my daughter's bed. I opened my eyes, and a tall, dark figure with a man's face stood above me. I wondered if my eyes were playing tricks on me, and I laid there for a moment peering up at it. I reached for my phone to turn on my flashlight, and immediately, it vanished.

My daughter, Anna, had been telling my husband, Liam, and me that there was a man in her room, but we didn't believe her. We were moved into the apartment for only a couple of weeks, and she refused to sleep in her own room and told us a tall scary man would come out of her closet and touch her while she was in bed.

I remembered being scared of the dark as a child, so my concern for this was little. However, my irritation for her insisting that she slept in me and Liam's bed was much more than a little. She struggled for weeks to go to sleep in her room and through the night. If she wasn't standing by my bedside telling me that she was scared, she was telling me that she peed the bed (which was out of her character). Trying to maintain sensitive to her 2-and-a-half-year-old heart and mind, I tended to her needs as best as I could. The night I woke up with the man standing over me was the first night I started to believe her.

The next night, Liam slept in Anna's room with her, and so did our dog, Pablo. Pablo seemed to do the trick for a while. As long as he slept in the room with her, she seemed to be unbothered.

Before long, what we thought was a ghost problem went away and it was no longer a concern when I separated from Liam and took Anna to Michigan where we stayed with my mom for ten months. Liam remained in the apartment during this time, and he slept downstairs on the couch, leaving the entire upstairs space to what we referred to at the time as a "ghosty".

We returned to live with Liam at the apartment at the end of those ten months, and immediately when we arrived, ghosty was back. Pablo the guard beagle assumed his place as a watch dog in Anna's room, but he didn't keep ghosty away for long this time. One evening, Pablo wined and barked from across the hall, and Anna shuffled into our room to my bedside. "Mama," she said, "The man's back in my room."

When I woke up the following morning, I was already thinking about the next night. *What do you do when your child is telling you that something is in her room? What do you tell her to do?*

After talking with my family members about it, I put my foot down that night, and I decided to show her that we don't give in or be afraid of things, especially evil. I wanted to make this a learning lesson and support her in the process, so I put her to bed and fell asleep in her room with her. I put a little cross that I bought for my grandma as a gift on her dresser, said a prayer, and went to bed. At some point in the night, I woke up and made my way into me and Liam's bedroom and fell back asleep.

A little while later, I woke up again and reached for my phone. It was 3 a.m. I looked across the hall into Anna's room, and immediately fear pulsed through my body. In the dim light from Anna's night light, a tall black figure draped over her bed and touched her back. In a state of panic, I jumped out of bed, flipped on the lights, and ran into her room. I scooped her up in my arms, and I ran back into my bedroom. I placed Anna between Liam and I and pulled the covers up high.

I laid in bed and my heart was beating so fast I could hear its pulse in my ears. *So much for teaching Anna to not be afraid,* I thought to myself. Still trying to process what I had just seen, after a few moments, I slowly let down the covers and looked across the hallway into Anna's room again.

With Anna safely between us, the man stood at the end of her bed again, but this time, he had a baby with him. At first, the man appeared to be taking care of the baby as it played and danced with it at the end of the bed, but suddenly, this changed. The dancing turned into violent blows to the baby, one after another. After several hits, it picked the baby up again and danced. This was followed again by hitting. I watched in awe across the house in bed as this occurred. I'm not sure how long I watched this happen, but at some point, I nudged Liam to wake him up. I pointed toward Anna's room and whispered, "Look!" I looked for his response when he looked into Anna's room. For the first time ever, I saw fear in his eyes. After a few seconds, he looked at me and said, "It's nothing," and rolled over to go back to sleep.

If there was one thing I knew, it was that what was happening across the hallway was not *nothing*, and I was going to make a point of that. Desperate to show that I was not crazy or seeing things, I grabbed my phone and recorded the man dancing with and hitting the baby. Needless to say, I didn't sleep for the rest of the morning.

The next morning, I showed Liam the video. Like the night before, he had nothing to say about it. All he said was, "Leave it alone."

I texted my mom and sent her the video. I didn't know what to do. *What does someone do when they have a ghost living with them?* If it were simply showing up once in a while, I'd say leave it alone too, but there was no way I was going to continue letting my daughter be touched by a ghost in her room until we moved out.

Liam refused to talk about it, so I was forced to handle the situation by myself. I spoke with my mom over the phone and came to the conclusion that our lease on the apartment only had a month and a half left, so letting Anna sleep in our room until we moved would be the best choice.

The next night, Anna did just that, and she slept in me and Liam's bedroom. I closed the door to her room, and we all went to bed. That night, nothing particularly crazy happened. Anna camped in her mini tent on our floor and was sound asleep, but my husband and I couldn't seem to sleep. We both woke up with muscle pains and cramps that we assumed were from working out at the gym, but for no reason at all we were wide awake at 3 a.m.

About an hour later, we found ourselves sitting on the couch downstairs watching NCIS. Trying to make the most out of my time, I pulled out my computer and tried to do some homework. There was no way I was leaving Anna upstairs alone, so I made Liam carry her downstairs to sleep on the couch next to him.

Once downstairs, I sat on the couch writing a paper for school when I felt a cold sensation on the top of my right hand around 5 a.m. Not thinking much of it, I continued writing my paper. I grew a little irritated by the feeling on my hand because it wouldn't go away. Thinking that what I was feeling had something to do with post workout muscle soreness or a small strain of some sort, I began to wonder if I was dehydrated and needed some water and electrolytes in my body. I made my way to the kitchen to get a Powerade from the refrigerator and continued my homework, and when I sat back down, what felt like a firm hand gripped my bicep. I was startled by this as I knew the feeling of a muscle cramp and a muscle spasm very well. This was not that. Something was grabbing me. It felt like a real person was grabbing my arm tightly.

I sat for a moment in my thoughts trying to collect myself. All that came to mind was the conversation I had had with my daughter about not being afraid. I sat up straight, looked at my word document on my laptop, and continued to write.

It's one thing to not be afraid, but it is another to be afraid and act like you're not. Again, like the night before, I felt like my heart was beating so fast that I could hear it, but I stayed firm in my seat and did not flinch. Although I didn't move and did not outwardly acknowledge that anything was happening, I imagine that what I thought was a ghost at the time knew exactly what I was thinking and what I was feeling as it was against my skin feeling me tremble in fear. Where I had previously been typing and working on my computer just moments before, as soon as it grabbed my bicep, the typing stopped. I sat still, frozen looking at my computer screen, body shaking.

I looked up slowly at Liam who was mesmerized by the TV, and just as I was about to tell him that something was touching me, it touched my cheek. I must have looked like something was terribly wrong, because when my husband glanced over at me and saw me looking at him, I saw fear in his face. "What's wrong?" he asked.

I was at a loss for words. I swallowed the lump in my throat, and I replied, "Is waffle house open?"

Chapter 2: Strangled By Something Invisible

"I told you not to fuck with it, and you just had to go taking a video of it!" Liam said to me.

"What did you expect me to do, just let it continue to mess with our daughter and for you to think I'm crazy?"

"I knew you weren't crazy. I just already knew what would happen if we fucked with it."

****

I was silent on the way to Waffle House. Once we were seated and ordered, I told Liam what had happened. He was furious. Not much was said after I told him what had happened in the living room. Just like me, he was scared, and he didn't want to admit it.

We were tired from our lack of sleep that night, so we went home and took a nap. During the day, our home was peaceful. No mysterious and unwanted sounds were heard, no objects were moved, and nothing touched us. When we woke up from our nap, I felt refreshed, but I was already thinking about the evening time. *What would tonight be like?*

I decided that we would sleep downstairs that night. I knew that Liam was bothered by what was going on too because he didn't even hesitate to ask why or argue when I told him that Anna and I were sleeping in the living room that night. He just came along with us.

Anna camped out on the living room floor in her mini tent and foldable bed and was asleep by 7:30. Again, Liam and I sat on the couch and watched NCIS, and I pulled out my laptop to do homework.

Although it hadn't stopped anything before, I closed all the doors upstairs and didn't plan on going back up there until the next morning. A little while later, while I was sitting on my laptop, I heard the ear piercing and unforgettable sound of Anna's door opening. Her door was slightly too big for the frame, so when it was opened, the door made a particular grinding sound. Sitting on the couch, I heard this noise come from upstairs. I looked at the clock. It was 8:00 p.m.

Within seconds, cold pressure laid itself on my hand again. Just like that morning. I began to panic. *What could I do?* As I sat in fear on the couch, it grabbed my bicep again.

Its grip was so firm that it hurt my arm terribly. Feeling desperate and hopeless, I closed my eyes to pray, but when I closed my eyes, I jumped out of my skin. If you've ever closed your eyes in the daylight or in a room with the lights on, you'd understand what I mean when I say that from behind your eyelids, your view is not completely dark. With the light from my computer and TV screen immediately in front of my eyes and the living room lights on, when I closed my eyes, the view under my eyelids was dark grey at best.

When I closed my eyes to pray, the silhouette of a black figure with bright red eyes and a cringy smile clung to my arm on the right side of my body. Before saying a word, I opened my eyes, and immediately, what felt like an ice cube ran from my arm, up my shoulder to the back of my neck. Pressure began to crush my neck, and I couldn't breathe. Gasping for air on the couch, I began to panic. I couldn't say a word, there were no fingers that I could pry off of my neck. I could only sit silently as I was strangled by something invisible. Ghosty wasn't a ghost at all; ghosty was a demon.

I looked at Liam who was still glued to the TV across the living room. He had no idea what was happening, and I couldn't get a word out to say his name. *This is the end*, I thought. *I'm going to die.* Still struggling to breathe and pressure still crushing my neck, I jumped to my feet and ran out the front door. As I ran through the door, the pressure stopped, and I could breathe.

I stood bent over with my hands on my knees under the moon and the stars breathing like I just finished running the 400-meter dash or was pulled to the surface after almost drowning in a lake. After a few seconds, I turned around to see Liam standing at the edge of the door. "What are you doing?" he asked.

"I…. I'm…. I'm not going back in there!" I gasped.

A few minutes later, we were all in the car, even Pablo. Anna was sleeping in her car seat, Pablo was lying down in the back seat next to her, and Liam didn't say a word. He didn't ask one question.

After a few minutes of disbelief, tears ran down my face, and I sobbed uncontrollably. We drove around Beaufort for about 20 minutes before Liam asked gently, "What happened?"

I told him what happened and explained to him about the black figure with red eyes. Without saying a word, he drove us home. He parked the car in the driveway and went inside. From the driveway, I could see all the lights, one by one, turn on inside the house. I called my grandma, who I knew was an avid Christian and worshiper of Jesus, and I told her what happened. She prayed for me over the phone and told me to not be afraid (easier said than done. It's not like you can just throw a punch at something like that.) "If it messes with you again," she said, "Call on the name of Jesus, and it will flee. It has to."

****

A little while later, after Liam turned all the lights on inside, I opened the front door and went inside. Carrying Anna, I shut the door behind me and looked around across the living room. *It looked normal.* Just then, Liam came walking down the stairs. "Pack a bag," he said.

We left Anna sleeping in the living room again, and we went upstairs to pack. I opened a bag and started throwing clothes into it. I didn't pay attention to what I was putting in it, I just wanted to leave as fast as possible.

Liam walked downstairs, and I was alone packing Anna's bag in our bedroom. Immediately, I felt the presence of the demon against my body. It stood on my back side like it was peering over my shoulder trying to see what I was doing. I felt like I was standing with my back facing an open freezer.

An all-encompassing fear took over me. Waiting for it to grab ahold of my throat again, my entire body shook in fear and my legs visibly wobbled back and forth. Like my grandma told me, I called on the name of Jesus. "In the name of Jesus, I rebuke you Satan," I said. It didn't work. Feeling frustrated and stupid, I said, "Thank you, Jesus." Nothing. "Please help me, Jesus." The cold sensation on my backside only grew closer and more intense. I could feel what felt like breathing in my ear. Chills covered my body. Beginning to panic again, I grabbed my phone and called my grandma.

"Grandma!" I said quickly "The thing is back, and it won't leave me alone! I don't know what to do!" She prayed, and immediately, it was gone. She used the same words I did (and then some), and it just went away. Just like that. When she was done, she told me to put on some Christian music until we left the house. The phone call ended, I finished packing, and we left.

We started driving around 10:30 that night to Indiana to visit Liam's family. What we didn't know until a month later when we returned to the apartment and talked to our neighbor who shared an adjoining wall with us was that when we drove away that night, cupboards and bedroom doors slammed all across the house when we left. The walls sounded like someone was banging on them, and the noise was so loud that she thought someone broke into our apartment.

It had tried to kill me, and I got away alive. It didn't like that at all.

Chapter 3: Brave

We spent the next month traveling and visiting our families. No one seemed to understand what I went through in the apartment. My muscles were sore where the demon grabbed and strangled me. It was painful to even touch my muscles gently, and they felt like they were bruised, but there was nothing to show. Although Liam had seen the video and experienced some of the spooky things that went on there, I could tell he questioned my sanity and mental health. Everyone did. Including myself.

At some point in our stay away from South Carolina, we had to plan to go back. Our lease was up at the end of the month, and we needed to pack our belongings and get ready to move to North Carolina. I dreaded this. The thought of setting foot back in that apartment sent shivers down my spine, let alone for an extended period of time to put our things in boxes and pack up a U-Haul trailer.

****

When we returned to the apartment, the house was cold, and dead spiders were scattered throughout the house. The steps of the stairs had dead spiders lining the railing, and they laid only on my side of the bed, almost forming the shape of a human body.

My grandma told me to pray when I got to the apartment, so I did. I didn't really know what to say, but I did it anyway. And then I got to packing. Nothing spooky happened on the first day. We packed the house, left it around 6 p.m., and then spent the night at a hotel in the evening. However, the next day, I was at the apartment alone with Anna when a package came to the front door. I picked the package up and closed the door behind me. Still standing in front of the door, I pulled the seal from the envelope and looked inside. Immediately, like the time I was packing clothes in my bag after I was strangled, I felt the demon standing behind me. A cold sensation started at my calves, ran up the back of my body, and hovered over my shoulders as if someone was peering into the package with me. It was curious about what was in the package. Sage.

Liam's family friends insisted that burning sage kept ghosts and evil spirits away and sent it to us in the mail. I wasn't planning on actually using it, but when I felt the demon on my back looking into the package with me, I quickly changed my mind. Not knowing anything about it, I opened YouTube on my phone, watched a video about how to use it, and walked around the house burning sage and saying the Lord's Prayer.

Wherever I walked in the apartment, the demon went with me on my back. Up the stairs, in the bedrooms, down the stairs, and in the kitchen. This continued for a while, and at some point, it went away. Most of our belongings were inside the U-Haul trailer at this point. Simple things needed packed, and a deep clean needed to take place. I bent down under the kitchen sink to grab Windex and paper towel when I heard a paralyzing, familiar sound coming from upstairs. I froze when I heard the sound of Anna's bedroom door opening. This was followed by the whizzing of the doorstop back and forth.

I looked down at the clock; it was about 3:30 in the afternoon. That was enough packing and cleaning for the day. I told Anna it was time to go, and before we left, I walked up the stairs into her bedroom. I passed through the door that was now open that I had left shut, and I moved the door so I could reach behind it. Bending down to the floor, I grabbed the doorstop and ripped it off the wall. Hopefully the landlord wouldn't see that it was gone.

That evening, Liam stopped by the apartment. It was about 9 o'clock when he went to leave the apartment, and just before he was about to leave, a pair of cold hands grabbed his upper arms and squeezed him tightly. With a lot of effort, he lifted his arms and broke the grip of the demon and freed his body. Jumping up off of the floor where he'd been sitting, he pointed at the stairs and yelled, "Go upstairs where you belong, and leave my family alone!"

After a few seconds, Liam stood at the bottom of the stairs when he heard Anna's door slam closed. He believed me now. I wasn't insane, I wasn't hallucinating, and I wasn't crazy.

The next morning, we left South Carolina for good. Early in the morning, I finished sweeping and vacuuming the floors, and I stood at the front door looking into the living room. It was empty, and the smell of bleach and lemons filled the air. I grabbed the broom and vacuum that sat by the door and closed it behind me. I closed the door like I was closing a chapter of a book. A bad book. Little did I know that it would get much worse, and we were just getting started.

Chapter 4: Afraid of The Dark

The next few months were difficult. Although we had left the demon behind in our apartment, life seemed to treat us poorly. Nothing seemed to go our way. Liam's transfer from the Marine Corps to the Army had many complications, and Anna's behavior and bedtime habits reflected the trauma she'd been though. I didn't tell anyone (even Liam), but I was struggling. I mean, really struggling. My experience in the apartment had left me debilitated. Although we left the apartment, the experience and trauma that had occurred hadn't seemed to leave me yet, and having been touched by something so unrealistic and evil like a demon, I felt like I had a disease. This wasn't anything like the trauma of getting bit by a dog, injured in a car accident, or hit by a parent. There were so many more uncertainties about the demon. I had no idea where it was at, what happened to it, or if it would come back.

Seeing a shadow in the midst of the day run across the wall from the daylight outside the window would make racing anxiety flood my chest, and as morning drew closer to evening time, the stress and anxiousness I experienced grew more intense.

I couldn't talk to anyone about my experience with the demon because as soon as I mentioned it, I could see the gears turning in their head as thoughts and opinions of disbelief and concern churning around. Instead, I managed my emotions with exercise. One-hour gym sessions turned into a three-hour gym sessions, and a short run turned into an hour-long run. Along with exercise, I fixated on food and caffeine and forged a path through the day with them. This only worked so much, though.

After overloading my system with food, caffeine, and exercise, I still felt intense emotional discomfort. I often looked up at the top of the fridge at an unopened bottle of New Riff Kentucky Straight Bourbon that was given to Liam as a gift when he left the Marine Corps and wondered what magic it might do for me. Knowing my dad's family history with alcohol, I used what willpower I had left to keep away from this. It peered down at me almost humorously every night as I drowned in anxiety until the early hours of the morning. Sometimes, a medicine cup full of NyQuil did the trick and put me to sleep for a little while.

****

I did this during the next phase of our lives in North Carolina. There, Liam was often away at training or sleeping in the field, which meant long, sleepless nights by myself and a room full of shadows that taunted me. Like an alarm was set in my mind, I woke up every morning at 3 a.m. I ended up sleeping with the lights on and falling asleep if I was lucky enough. After months of this, I was exhausted and lonely.

Like clockwork one morning, I woke up at 3 a.m. and laid in bed desperate for some relief for my fear and anxiety. A tree moved outside my window which sent a shadow dancing across the wall in my room. The sight of this took my breath. I felt like I could puke. This was enough. I turned on the lights and flopped back down on the bed.

Turning sideways like a baby, I cried. I didn't just cry, I wept. *Why did this happen to me? I knew no one else who had been strangled by a demon. Why me?*

After a long time of rationalized self-pity, I heard my grandma's voice in my head. "When you go into the apartment, turn on the Christian music. It will help."

I decided to try this in an attempt to sleep. Clueless about what to listen to and in the midst of my chaotic drowsiness, I opened the YouTube app on my phone, typed "Church" in the search bar, and I clicked on the first thing that popped up: Elevation Church.

Now, I can't tell you what the sermon was about or what it was called, but one thing I do remember is that I slept. For the first time in about eight months, I slept. With the light still on and blaring in my face at 3 a.m., I slept with Elevation

Church content on repeat in my ear until 9 o'clock that morning when Anna jumped on me to wake me up.

"What are you listening to, Mama?" she asked. *That was a good question, I didn't know either.* Leaving my phone running on the bed, we went outside and took Pablo for his morning walk. After we made breakfast, I found my phone still playing on my bed. After the sleep I got that morning, I was curious as to the magic that I was listening to. I turned on the shower and continued to listen.

If you've ever been really hungry and had to wait a while for something to eat, you'd know the feeling you get when you eat something really good. You're so hungry that you could just eat and eat and eat until your stuffed like a turkey on Thanksgiving. And then, when you have room, you do it all again. This is how these sermons felt. Standing in the shower, I listed to Steven Furtick preach and ask me, "Are you a bird in a bowl trying to fly?"

My answer was yes. It didn't matter what part of my life we were talking about. I was a bird in a bowl flapping my wings and trying to take off but going nowhere. I couldn't even manage to get sleep at night.

In desperate need of some kind of relief to my daily anxiety and fear. The sound of Steven Furtick's voice in my ears preaching the word of God came to be the only thing that helped me. Day and night, a sermon was playing. Sometimes, I listened to the same one over and over and over. I didn't care, though. It helped, and I got something new out of it every time.

I found out quickly that when a person experiences trauma that occurred on a spiritual level, it can't be addressed simply at a physical level. You have to match the offense and fix it at a spiritual level. I tried everything from journaling to yoga, and the only thing that made me feel better for more than five minutes at a time was the word of God.

The word of God was somewhat a new concept to me at the time. I had always believed in God, but I didn't know Him. I wasn't raised in a church, and I felt silly praying. The damage from my run-in with the demon forced me to get closer to God, and with the amount of time I spent watching sermons and praying, I got closer to Him very quick. This became my normal everyday life. In fact, on most days, it was the only way I felt that I could keep going.

Chapter 5: *Are you going to be afraid?*

Almost a year later, I found myself in relationship with Jesus, praying to him day and night, and feeling much better. My sleep habits were better, and so was my anxiety. Rather than going to God and watching sermons simply for survival, I was able to enjoy them both.

Around the same time, we found ourselves moving to Fort Leavenworth, Kansas where Liam worked as a corrections officer at one of the prisons on base. We arrived in the summer and were greeted by the extreme heat that proved to feel hotter than the low country in South Carolina. We moved into a three-bedroom townhouse on base, and shortly after arriving, our new neighbors started complaining about noise coming from our extra bedroom at 8 o'clock every night.

At the time, the room was filled with boxes that were yet to be unpacked from our move from North Carolina. Needing only two bedrooms, the room was temporarily being used as a storage spot until we finished unpacking. We kept the door to it closed and only entered it when we needed something from it.

When the neighbors started complaining about the noise, I thought they were being petty. I exchanged phone numbers with the woman, Samantha, and told her to text me when she heard the noise so we could pinpoint exactly what was making a disturbance for them.

As time passed, she texted me when she heard the noise, but we heard nothing. Usually, she would text me and insist that someone was banging on the wall, but everyone, including our dogs, were downstairs.

At this point, the best of me wanted to believe that the demon chapter was behind us and closed, but what made me uneasy is that it occurred at the same time every night at 8 o'clock. This made me think back to the time I heard Anna's bedroom door open at 8'oclock before the demon strangled me.

As weeks passed, Samantha continued to text me and let me know that someone was banging on the wall almost every night. I wondered if I'd ever hear the banging she was hearing. Sure enough, I did eventually.

****

Bang, bang, bang. Pablo's ears went up from across the living room. My heart sank into my stomach and turned upside down. Then again, bang, bang, bang. I pulled out my phone to check the time. It was 8 p.m.

I sat on the couch for a moment beginning to panic. *What do I do? What do I do? God, what do I do?*

In the midst of my mind racing as fear washed over me and I remembered the red eyes of the demon and the way it strangled me, the gentlest and quietest yet most assertive and directive voice in my head responded with a question, "Well, are you going to be afraid of it?"

This stopped me in my tracks. I was finally in a place where I thought I had gotten over the trauma from the demon in South Carolina. I didn't want to go back down that road again. I didn't understand why God would let it back into our lives. I thought about this question for a moment. Although I was afraid, and God already knew I was, the right answer was *no*. So, I asked God, "What do I do?" Without hesitation, God told me to tell it to leave.

This was not at all what I wanted to do. I wanted to leave, not to mention that it never listened to anything I told it before. I was so nervous that my airway felt like it was closing up and my knees were shaking. I walked, step after step, one foot after the other, up the stairs and to the door of the extra bedroom. I stood there for a moment contemplating my next move, but before I could change my mind, I pushed the door open as fast as I possibly could. "Get out!" I yelled.

"This isn't your house; in the name of Jesus, I command you to leave me and my family alone."

Knees still shaking and half expecting something that looked like it was from a movie scene to happen, I stood in the room waiting for something to touch me or for pressure to crush my neck, but nothing happened.

****

The next morning, I was sitting at my desk typing on my computer in the living room when I felt a familiar touch on my hand. I could recognize the feeling anywhere. Like a year and a half earlier, something was touching me. Trying to be calm and brave, I tried to ignore it and prayed to God silently in my head. I continued about my business as if nothing was happening, and like a pair of cold doctor hands, the demon gently stroked my forehead and remained close so

I could feel its presence. Again, I felt like I was standing next to an open freezer door holding an icepack on my head. *You've got to be kidding me*, I thought. *What happened to telling it to leave?*

Terrified, I continued to silently pray in my head. *God, what do I do? I don't want this.* I didn't dare close my eyes.

I started to panic. All I could imagine was that the same thing was going to happen again, and a pair of invisible hands would begin to strangle me. Grabbing my coffee cup and starting to stand up from my chair, the same question from the night before caught me in my tracks. *Are you going to be afraid of it?*

This was God, again, and He was calling me out on my fear. Setting my cup back down on the desk, I knew He was right. Desperately wanting to walk away, put Anna's shoes on her, and leave the house, I did quite the opposite.

I took a deep breath. "I can feel you," I said. This was met with an ice-cold touch on my right cheek. Continuing to sound crazy and talk out loud to something invisible, I said, "I thought I told you to leave."

Nothing.

Waiting for some sort of response to this, I said to it, "I don't know who you are, what you want, or why you're here, but one thing I do know for sure is that you're only here if God lets you." At this, it moved from clinging to my right side and touching my face to covering my back. It draped over me like a cloak. After a few seconds, a cold and concentrated pressure pushed against my shoulder blades. It almost felt like I was wearing a backpack.

My demeaner remained calm, but inside, I was terrified. Again, as much as I tried to fake it with my outward actions, the demon was touching me, so it could feel my heart racing and body shaking.

Mustering up some last words from my throat that felt like it was stuck closed, I ended the conversation with, "So, if God wants you living here, we mind as well get used to each other." At this, the pressure on my back intensified like two ice cubes being pressed against my skin.

I stood up from my desk and went to get my daughter. Thoughts were racing in my mind. *I am going crazy? Is this what being schizophrenic is like? Am I hallucinating? Was that the demon, or am I having muscle spasms? I should probably pull out my phone and google symptoms of cold sensations on skin. Muscle spasms too. Where's Anna? I need to get out of here for a while. I thought I prayed for it to*

leave last night. It listened to Liam when he told it to leave.
Why is it still…

My thoughts were interrupted. From downstairs, I could hear Anna's sweet little four-year-old voice. "Student, sit down!" she said. She was playing school. I walked up the stairs and into her room and the sight of her innocent and smiling face automatically filled me with joy and hope.

Knowing full well what she was doing and seeing that her room full of stuffed animals sitting in perfect rows with books and papers in front of them, I asked her, "What are you doing, baby?"

Handing me a card, she replied, "I'm teaching. Want to play?"

"I was thinking we could go play in the sand. What do you think?" She jumped up and down screaming "Yes!"

repeatedly and ran down the stairs. I reached for her light switch, turned the light off, walked out of the room, and followed her. Lifting up the card she handed me, I stopped at the top of the stairs when I read it. It was a prayer card that I bought from the Dollar Tree in North Carolina a year earlier. In pretty pink writing, it read, *"Be still and know I am God."*

****

Later that night, after putting Anna to bed, I walked into my bedroom and closed the curtains. The neighbors' back porch light was glaring at me through the window. Liam was on the night shift working at the prison, so I had the king bed all to myself. I sat on the edge of the bed, slipped my shirt over my head, and dropped it on the floor. I bent down and reached to pull my socks off when I was stopped by the familiar feeling on my shoulder blades that I felt that morning. I picked up my shirt and slipped it back on. I walked over to my closet, put on a pair of sweatpants, and climbed into bed. I pulled the blanket up high enough so that only my eyes peered out over the top of them. As I laid in bed, I felt it touch my forehead.

That was it, I had enough. Again, I walked over to the closet and put on a sweatshirt. I pulled the hood over my head, turned a light on, and played an Elevation Church sermon on my phone. I climbed in bed, and like a child, I pulled the covers over my head. Although I could still feel the pressure on my back, being in sweats and covered by blankets made me feel safe. I said a prayer, asked God to take it out of my life, and went to bed.

****

This became normal for me. The demon would show up in the middle of my day while I did random things in the house, touch me, and move things in the house on a regular basis. The more it happened, the more desensitized I got to it. It was my new normal. I continued to seek God, ask for his help and guidance, and didn't tell anyone about what was happening. Scared of being called crazy, I kept it my secret.

Liam was working an unusual number of hours in the prison, and after a lot of nights with the demon and without him, one evening when he wasn't working, we climbed into bed together at the same time. Pulling back the covers, I got underneath them wearing sweatpants and a hoodie, and he looked at me confused, "Why are you wearing that?"

Unable to admit out loud to him anything that had gone on in the past few months, all I could get out was, "They make me feel safe." At my response, I saw concern on his face, but also confusion. He'd been working night shift until recently, and we had not seen each other besides in passing for a few months. Trying to settle his mind, I said, "It's been hard sleeping here every night without you."

Relief ran over his face when I said this. "Well, I'm here now, and I'm done with nights next week." I scooted closer to him and moved under his arm and covered my back with it. He made me feel safe.

****

A few hours later, I woke up on the other side of the bed when I heard noises coming from Liam. I rolled over and saw his arm sticking straight up in the air. With his other arm, he stroked his arm back and forth slowly while making a noise that sounded like he was chewing and licking his lips.

"Are you okay?" I asked him. Thinking he couldn't hear me, I poked his arm and asked him again. He was sleeping. From the other side of the bed, fear started to flood me as I watched him continue to rub his arm that was sticking straight up in the air. Every few seconds, he made a noise and then went back to making chewing sounds again. *This isn't normal*, I thought. Where he had been my safe haven from my new unwanted friend just hours before, I then wanted to be away from him.

I reached over again and tried to wake him up. I shook him many times before he opened his eyes. "What are you doing?" I asked. He looked at me confused. "Why is your arm just sticking straight up in the air?"

He turned over and went back to sleep. I laid in bed for a while thinking about this, and as I was about to finally fall back asleep, Liam's arm went up in the air again, and again, he started to rub it with his other hand. Something

didn't feel right. I just had a gut feeling about it. Deciding

to pray for him, I reached over and touched his arm before I

began. It was ice cold, like a freezer.

Chapter 6: Simon Says

Some things you have to go through to understand fully what the experience is like. This is the case for living with a demon. I can't describe to you my experience living with the demon in full detail the way I want to, and this is for two reasons. First, because the experience is so indescribable and incomparable to any other event I've ever experienced.

Putting it into words shrinks it down into a category that downplays every part of it. It wasn't one significant event that occurred on a physical level. It was a reoccurring, compound, long-term experience that occurred on physical, mental, and spiritual levels. Rather than a significant event of trauma like one or a couple instances of abuse, it was abuse that occurred every day for an extended period of time, and in between significant acts of abuse, it was rationalized and taught, each lesson scaffolded one top of another, like learning math. It's too long, complicated, and complex to describe accurately. To really understand it, you have to live it, which isn't something I'd wish on anyone.

Second, if I could tell you each detail of how it communicated with me, what its hands felt like when it touched my skin, and the ideas if put into my head day in and day out, I would. If I did, though, I would spiral down the rabbit hole of anxiety attacks and PTSD symptoms after the first page of writing and not be able to continue further.

In this chapter, I describe to you the most basic, sugarcoated version of my experience with the demon and explain the ways it tried to communicate and control me. The little bit I am able to make sense of and describe is only because of a lot of Lexapro, a lot of coping strategies, and mostly, a lot of Jesus. Perhaps, though, it's better that I leave out the dreadful details anyways.

****

After I opened the door upstairs when I heard the knocking, I was visited by the invisible freezer demon daily. It would randomly grab me or show up on my back, and it visited me when I went to bed and in the middle of the night. It ticked my feet, stroked the side of my face and my hair, and gave me no personal space. It wiggled the doorstops, and I'd rip them off the wall. Often, I'd be cooking in the kitchen, driving in my car, working on my laptop at my desk, or watching TV when it would casually show up and interrupt what I was doing by grabbing me.

The first thing I always did when this happened was pray, and then I ignored it. I tried rebuking it in Jesus' name and listening to Elevation Church sermons, but no matter what I did, it continued to happen. It was not going away.

I often started to question my sanity, but God would gently remind me that I wasn't crazy. He reminded me of the video I took of the demon in Anna's room and Liam's interaction with it in South Carolina. He reminded me of the moving doorstops that whizzed back and forth by themselves, the doors that opened and closed, the fact that the neighbors heard the banging upstairs too, and the sight of

Pablo's ears perking up at the sound of the pounding coming from the upstairs. These memories gave me the shred of hope I needed to remember that I wasn't crazy and that I WAS living with a demon from hell. Sometimes, just to keep my head up and moving forward, I'd affirm myself out loud and say, "I'm not crazy."

As the demon continued to touch me and grab me and make itself known to me, I continued to pray and ask God to take it away. After seeing no change, I grew angry. A lot of what if scenarios played out out in my mind, and I wondered if I would live the rest of my life with the demon. As my confusion and interactions with the demon started occurring more frequently, I noticed a parallel with Liam. When I wasn't feeling its presence, Liam acted crazy. It wasn't until much later that I realized that when it wasn't messing with me, it messed with him. It kept him up, influenced his behavior, and made him mean. Liam's memory started going away at some point, he busted out in anger randomly and in simple conversations, slept any time he could during the day, and was awake at night. If he was able to sleep at night, his arm stuck straight up in the air while he slept and he shouted random words in his sleep. At the very least, it was scary.

After a few months, I started noticing that the demon was touching me at particular times. There were patterns and trends to when it was touching me. It was getting my attention. In conversations, while watching TV or reading, through parenting, or whatever else I was doing, I grabbed me when it wanted me to pay attention to what was going on around me.

At first, I did my best to ignore the touches that came across as alerts, but as they occurred, it grew difficult to not pay attention to them. It was like trying to ignore someone that you know at the grocery store and you don't want to interact with.

I first noticed this when it started grabbing me every time I saw a dog or heard a dog. For example, when my dogs would come into the room it grabbed me to get my attention, and it also did this when I heard dogs barking outside, when a dog showed up in a TV show on the TV, or when my daughter would run around on all fours in the house pretending that she was a dog. After it established the connection for the dog, it would move onto the next thing. It did this with many things like urine, water, maple leaves, nails, cages, tables, the words upside down and backwards, rainbows, fruits, bees, hair clips, and many other things.

As time continued, it alerted me of repeating numbers like 444, 333, or 2121. For example, I'd be sitting on the couch or driving in the car when I would feel it grab me, and

I'd look up and see 12:12 on the clock or 555 on a license plate. Eventually, it started grabbing me when I felt certain emotions. For example, when I felt scared, it would grab me, and after I noticed this connection, it then started grabbing me only when I felt peaceful.

I was confused by all of these alerts and the associations it was trying to reinforce. Remembering how it once tried to strangle me in South Carolina, I didn't understand why it was friendly now. I didn't understand why its demeaner changed. Regardless of its intentions and possible change of heart, I still wanted God to take it away. I prayed to him for help, I begged him on my knees to take it away from me every day. What I didn't realize until much later was that the demon was grooming me. It was trying to befriend me, win me over, and eventually, convince me it was God. After showing up in every part other part of my life, it started trying to communicate with me and touching me while I watched sermons, played worship music, prayed, and read the Bible.

As you can imagine, this was confusing. It was the same ice-cold touch that I'd been feeling the whole time and that strangled me in South Carolina. I started to ask God during my prayer time why it was showing up during the times I was trying to learn about or worship Him. I kept moving forward, asking God for guidance and help discerning what was Him.

To be honest with you, moving forward felt paralyzing. It's easy to write about it and talk about it now after it happened and simply say, "I kept moving forward." At the time, though, simply existing was difficult to do. I felt like I was living in a different world or an alternate reality, and I didn't know what was God and what was the demon.

Where most people are able to focus on daily life like their to-do list for the day, I was stuck in my head because of a clingy, manipulative demon. The presence of the demon in my life occurred so often at this point that it was impossible to ignore it, but I didn't want to make the wrong move. I didn't want to worship the devil, and I didn't want to disappoint God. The demon was disrupting my daily life to the point that I couldn't focus. I didn't feel normal, and I was quite aware that every time I talked to it, I looked crazy. In public and in front of my family, I acted as normal as I possibly could, but behind closed doors, it was game on. All I wanted was to get the demon off of me.

As if feeling the demon's ice-cold touches wasn't enough, at some point, it started talking to me. I could hear it in my head. Clear as day, it sounded like another voice in my head, and it often pretended to be God. I once heard a preacher tell a joke that talked about how to boil a frog. It said that when you boil a frog, you put the frog in cold water and slowly turn up the heat so the frog doesn't know it's being boiled. This is what the demon was doing to me. It put me in cold water and slowly turned up the heat. Once it desensitized me of its freezer hands, it started talking to me.

The demon's voice came into my head like a person coming onto a loudspeaker in a grocery store to dispatch an associate to the front. It told me what to do, said conflicting and confusing things, and try to show me different interpretations of the Bible. My relationship with God at this point moved from a matter of trust to a matter of survival. It rationalized itself as God, used compelling evidence, and used my beliefs and past experiences to confuse me and steer me away from Jesus and religion altogether.

One of the things it did was show me different interpretations of Bible stories and used them against Jesus. It broke Christianity into learning phases and told me that the 12 disciples were 12 different learning stages that lead to becoming like Jesus. It described them like grades in school or levels in a video game. It rationalized this with the reoccurring theme of music in the Bible. It further rationalized this by explaining how the 12 notes that make up a musical scale work together in order to make a song. It brought the idea of instruments and harmonies working together to create music and explained that this was the true meaning of tongues.

Eventually, it made associations with meanings and objects and activities that occurred in my surroundings. For example, it associated praying with washing and cleaning and when I saw soap, napkins, paper towel, brooms, wipes, and other cleaning supplies, it would tell me to pray and what to pray for. It also did this when I saw someone cleaning, while I cleaned, or when anything in my environment happened that dealt with some version of cleaning. It did this with almost every object in my environment. Water, food, clothing, and animals were all associated with commands or tasks. The fact that it told me to pray doesn't sound problematic, but it used this as a gateway to condition me to listen to it. It tried to tell me to do other things that were harmful or negative, and when I didn't listen, it started associating more and more things with positive commands it previously told me to do to take up my time and space in my mind and entangle my thoughts. Before I knew it, everything in my surroundings was associated with a command. I couldn't think straight because everything around me was constantly telling me to do something. I was like Pavlov's dogs, but drooling over everything not only the sound of a bell.

The last thing the demon did was what I refer to and describe now as magnification. Like sticking a magnifying glass over something that you want to see more clearly, what felt like a parallel version of this but in my mind started to occur. The voice, the associations that the demon previously made with objects, and other things in my surroundings were magnified. It was impossible to not notice it, and it consumed my attention and it put me into a mental state that I can only begin to describe as Euphoria. It felt like I was not in control of the part of my brain that I used to focus on things. The demon stole my ability to live in the present, and instead, I was living in my head and magnified and focused on things of its choice.

This went on for weeks, and it made life unbearable. I felt like I was standing in the middle of a crowd of people who were talking amongst themselves, and it was so loud I couldn't hear myself think or calm my inner self to form thoughts and make decisions.

When this happened, I begged God, multiple times a day, sometimes multiple times an hour, for help. I lived with sermons and Christian music playing on repeat, and I studied my Bible. When nothing changed, the demon told me that I was being punished for talking to it, it told me that God left me, and that I deserved what was happening to me. It filled my head with lies, told me that I would never get better, and slowly tried to convince me that I'd be better off dead. It blamed Jesus, called Jesus the devil, and fed me any information that it could to support this accusation.

Around this time, I got pregnant and lost my husband. I say I lost him, but I don't mean he actually died. I mean that one day without any warning, he left. He came home once a week to get clothes, but other than that, he was gone. He wouldn't talk to me or Anna, he wouldn't eat dinner with us, and he wouldn't sleep at home, and without any reason, his presence in our house was gone. There had been no argument, no significant events in our relationship or household besides my pregnancy; he simply absented himself from our lives silently. When I tried to talk to him, his memory clearly wasn't working. He turned mean, cold, and lifeless almost overnight. The few times I looked into his eyes during this time, it was as if his soul had left him. They were dark and lifeless.

One evening, after many weeks of Liam being away from home, he randomly decided to come home and sleep. I was lying in bed waiting for him to be done with his shower to go to bed when everything in my vision started to spin. I tried to stand up, but almost falling over, I laid back down and watched the ceiling spin. After a few minutes, Liam turned off the lights and climbed into bed next to me. Laying in the dark with my vision still spinning, I felt the demon's familiar touch on my skin. It tickled my feet, tampered with the curtains and shook the light that came in from outside, and laid next to me rubbing my head.

Laying in the dark that evening with everything spinning around me and the demon touching my forehead, it said to me, "I'm going to kill him."

The thing is, the devil can't kill you because he isn't in control. What he can do, though, is lie to you, manipulate your thoughts and reality to the point that you make choices that destroy your life and make you want to kill yourself. And this is exactly what he meant when the demon told me that it was going to kill Liam.

Our house and my marriage turned into what felt like a warzone. Refusing the love and protection of Jesus, my husband was tricked, manipulated, and smothered in every direction by the devil. It wasn't until much later that I found out that the voice that had been talking to me and masquerading itself as God and trying to push me away from Jesus was also in Liam's head and focusing on every flaw he had, influencing him to make choices that ruined his life, and convincing him to hurt and kill others around him.

After the demon told me he was going to kill Liam, I sat back and watch Liam destroy his life. I urged him to let Jesus into his life, but he refused. He became dangerous to be around, he made poor choices, spent a lot of money, slept with a lot of women, and forced Anna and I to leave and escape from our living conditions in the house with him. His body and mind became a breeding ground for hell. His personal and professional life suffered greatly, and eventually, I watched him become couchbound, debilitated, and want nothing more than to die.

Due to the demon's manipulation that was going on in my mind, the state of my mental health was poor, and I didn't have the strength or stamina to deal with Liam. I took Anna out of school one day, drove to Michigan, and visited my family for a week. No one at home knew what was going on. I didn't have the energy or the words to explain. All I knew was that I needed a break away from Kansas and Liam. We needed to be around family, and I desperately needed to be around others who knew Jesus.

During our visit, Anna and I went to my parents' church, and the voices disappeared. I could breathe, my head was clear, and the peace of God was on us. We stayed for a week, relaxed with family, and slowly made our way back to Kansas.

A few weeks after arriving back to Kansas from our visit with family, the demon, its voice, and its ice-cold touches came back again. I could feel it on my skin and heard it in my head. I prayed to God, rebuked the devil and the demon, and did my best to ignore its words in my head. As I continued to ignore and rebuke it, it continued to speak to me. It told me it was sorry, that it loved me, and that it was lonely. It came up with many reasons and excuses as to why it wanted to be with me and have me as its company. It didn't matter where I went, in the car, to the gym, or at home, it continued to speak to me. Eventually, as I continued to refuse speaking or interacting with it, it took on the connotation of stalker. It filled my head with sentences about how it could see me all the time and that it would always be with me.

At some point, it was almost as if the demon had enough of my unwillingness to participate in its games and it turned up the heat. Rather than hearing one voice, I started to hear multiple voices. The voices argued back and forth and tried to confuse me. The demon started to grab me more often and magnify the objects in my surroundings again. It was as if all the weapons that the demon had used over the past year were used against me at the same time and in the most intense forms. It felt like torture, and I wanted to die.

Eventually, the chaos in my head grew so intense that I could barely make it from one minute to the next. Everything inside felt like a war, and there was absolutely no break from the madness that was happening inside. Things that I previously did to distract or help cope with the voices like exercising, art, playing my ukelele, playing with my daughter, or going on a walk no longer worked for that purpose. The voices focused on control and related everything that was happening in my surroundings to the idea that religion and Jesus were controlling me. Things like cages and animals were used as a reference for being trapped by Jesus. I felt like I was drowning underwater and couldn't breathe. It was no longer a matter of getting through the day or distracting from it, it was a matter of pure survival. All I knew was that I needed help as soon as possible. I was reaching a point where I didn't think I could keep going and all voices except the voice of God were pointing toward the idea that it would be better to be dead than alive.

Chapter 7: Survive or Die

Eventually, my condition got so bad that I called my mom to ask her for help, but through my confusion and exhaustion, I couldn't get the right words out. As I talked to her over the phone, her words vibrated around in my head, the demon argued with everything she said, and my head felt like it was spinning as I tried to explain what was happening to me.

I could hear the concern in her voice as she tried to rationalize what I was going through with stress. "No, mom. You don't understand." I could hear the irritation in her voice when she responded. She was trying to understand, but I sounded crazy.

"There are voices in my head arguing and talking to me." I could hear her breathing from the other side of the phone. "It's like a war in my head." My mom is a wise woman who always has valuable insight, but at this, she didn't have much to say. After holding in what had been terrorizing me for more than a year up to this point, she had no idea what our conversation would be about when she picked up the phone.

"This isn't about mental health, Mom. It's about the demon." That's all I could coherently convey to her.

After a moment of silence, from the other end of the phone, I could tell she was desperately reaching deep down for any suggestion or advice to give me when she slowly asked, "Have you considered being baptized?"

****

Sometimes, when God speaks to you, there is no question about it whether or not its Him by how it hits you. At this moment, the word of God came through my mom to me in the middle of my confusion and the voices. I knew right then and there that I needed to be baptized.

****

"Let me contact my pastor and see if he would be available in the next few weeks," my mom said to me. Just the idea of living another day in the condition I was in was dreadful.

"No, mom." I blurted out. "I'm coming home now."

After I got off the phone with my mom, I started to pack bags to go visit Michigan. By this time, I was almost 8 months pregnant, so I grabbed all my maternity outfits and clothes for my daughter. I packed the car full, and got the dogs situated into the backseat of my little car.

When the car was all packed, I went inside to get Anna, and she met me at the bottom of the stairs and said, "Mama, I just saw someone walking around upstairs." My heart sank.

****

The car ride to Michigan was the longest 12 hours of my life. Voices argued in my head, spoke to me, and spoke to each other. My mind felt like I had been kidnapped and shoved in the backseat of a car while others were driving and yelling at each other. I prayed, played Christian music, sang and praised God at the top of my lungs with tears running down my face, called my mom and my grandma, and played I Spy with Anna, but nothing would make the voices go away. Anna must have thought I was crazy. At times, I didn't even know if we would make it all the way to Michigan.

My body was under such an extreme amount of stress that I was worried for my health and the health of my baby. I was hyperventilating, shaking, and felt like my heart was going to jump out of my chest. Looking back now, it's a miracle that I made it all that way in that physical and mental state, especially being pregnant.

When we finally reached Michigan, I was mentally and physically depleted. I waddled inside my mom's house, took care of Anna and our dogs, and waited for the evening to come. When I laid my head down on the pillow to sleep that night, my mind was still racing. I prayed to God and begged Him for rest. Voices still ran around and argued in my head. Finally, I pulled out a pocket Bible from my daughter's backpack and shoved it under my head in my pillowcase. With my ears laying on the hard surface of the Bible and the corner of it shoved into the side of my head, for the first time in a long time, it was quiet. I closed my eyes and didn't wake up until the morning.

When I woke up the next morning, the voices were back. The day couldn't go by fast enough. I was scheduled to talk to the paster in the evening at my mom's church, and all day, my surroundings magnified through my ears and eyes and into my brain. I could only hope that baptism would help. I walked around and existed at my mom's house like I was okay, but I felt like a zombie inside. I closed my eyes when I could, tried to tune out the chaos, and plugged my ears with my fingers, and did the only thing I knew to do: survive.

After what seemed like eternity, five o'clock finally came around, my mom drove me to the church. When we walked inside, immediately, the confusion and the voices were gone. I could breathe, and I could think. I met my mom's pastor, Pastor Harley, for the first time, and went into his office to talk to him and his wife, Cory, and explain my situation. I told him a light version of my story, and I explained the situation about the demon in the apartment in South Carolina and what had occurred most recently. Toward the end, I told him, "All I know is that I have a word from God, and it's to get baptized."

Where my mom, who is trained in psychology, jumped straight to the conclusion that what I was experiencing was a mental health crisis, Paster Harley had witnessed the presence of evil in his life too. When I talked to him, immediately, I knew God led me to the right place. Finally, someone who believed me and knew I wasn't crazy.

The baptism was organized the following day. Again, it was one of the longest days of my life. I slept with my head on a Bible again that night, but this time, it was a full-sized one that the pastor's wife gave me. My body was going through the motions the day of the baptism, but mentally, I was just along for the ride. The voices were so loud that eventually it felt like ringing in my ears.

That evening, I stood in the cold June water of Lake Missaukee in Northern Michigan. At some point, on the drive to the lake, the chaos in my mind stopped, and the

95

voices left. The Pastor Harley and Cory met us there, and we waded into the water up to our stomachs. We were met by my family who walked out on a dock where I was dipped into the water.

Afterward, we celebrated over my mom's lasagna, and for the first time, I gathered with people with a fresh and clear mind. I could talk and hear freely. Nothing magnified or echoed back to me. Where I had been walking around each day feeling like my head was 7 feet under water, I felt like I finally had been pulled out from the bottom of the ocean from drowning. I felt at peace.

The voices were gone, and it was as if the prison walls that had been enclosing my mind were knocked down. Nothing grabbed my arm or clung to my back. Nothing tried to tickle my feet or stroke my hair when I went to sleep at night, and for the first time in a long time, I felt free.

Chapter 8: Recovery

I wasn't prepared for the aftermath of the damage that was inflicted during my journey with the demon.

When you experience trauma or stress for such a prolonged period of time, it becomes your normal, and your tolerance for stress and unhealthy conditions simply increases with each day until your body finally reaches its limit. The morning following my baptism, I woke up and felt as if my body was detoxed or recovering from a severe illness or injury. I experienced a state of recovery that felt like the following days after being in a car accident, and my muscles and joints ached. My shoulders, back, and neck muscles ached, and my right knee hurt to the point of limping. Simple movements like getting in and out of my car and on and off the toilet were painful, and not just because I was pregnant.

Not only was my body sore, but it was like my brain was sore, tired, and worn out. It was like I had been subjected into an alternate reality for a year, taken out of it, and thrown into real-life without any transition period. Everything around me felt so real that it was overwhelming. It was as if my senses had been broken or working on a different level for so long that they didn't work properly anymore on a regular level. Now that the voices and the demon problem were gone, it was as if I was seeing, hearing, smelling, feeling, and tasting everything in overdrive. The silence of regular everyday life was overwhelming, and my body was stuck in survival mode. I was beyond thankful to be back in reality now, free from the grips of hell, no longer bound by the demon's freezer hands, and delivered by God, but I was now easily overwhelmed, I surrounded by triggers that reminded me of my trauma, my mind had been hardwired for survival, and almost everything around me was sending me into full blown anxiety attacks. I was experiencing symptoms and episodes of post-traumatic stress disorder.

****

Days following the baptism, I sat outside my mom's house under tall white pines in a hard wooden chair. My sunglasses dimmed the sunlight that peered through the branches, and wadded up paper towel plugged my ears and lessened my hearing of the birds chirping and the lawn mower I the distance. I pressed sap between my fingers and felt the stickiness of it cling between my fingers while I stared straight ahead. Cars whizzed by on the road, and the aroma of horse manure lingered in the air.

My mom pulled into the driveway, brought me over a sweet tea, and talked to me for a moment. "How are you doing?" she asked.

"Pretty good," I lied. From the outside, I probably just looked like a normal pregnant lady who was tired, but on the inside, I was suffering greatly. Everything around me felt like it was moving 100 miles per hour while I was stuck in place and unable to move. It was the kind of anxiety that takes the breath right out of your lungs and makes you think you're having a heart attack. My surroundings were constantly filled with triggers that elicited a survival response in my body that felt like an alarm was being set off.

Dogs, cages, nails, urine, water, heat, coldness, the smell of smoke, cooking, braids, washing, apples, grapes, hair clips, cookies, sunflowers, butterflies, maps, roads, certain songs, bugs, pinecones, and almost everything in between were all triggers for me. At any given time, at least one thing was in my surroundings that was triggering my anxiety, and I was constantly experiencing stress or anxiousness. My memory was failing to work, and things people were saying to me would go in one ear and out the other. It was another day in a different situation, and I was still trying to survive.

Stilling visiting my family in Michigan, I let my daughter run wild entertaining herself with bugs and animals while I sat in the chair completely depleted of energy and desperately needing rest. My stomach ached, and my baby kicked me in the ribs all day and night reminding me of her entrance world that was just weeks away. All I could think about was what mess of a life was waiting for me back in Kansas. I didn't want to go back.

****

After a conversation with my parents, I decided to move back home to Michigan. I drove back to Kansas for a couple days to take care of a few things, and at 33 weeks pregnant, I departed Kansas for Michigan with a car trunk full of belongs, Anna and my two dogs in the backseat, and 1,500 dollars in my bank account to live with my parents.

As we left Kansas and headed back to Michigan, I looked in the review mirror, and I saw tears flowing out of Anna's eyes. When my eyes met hers, she asked me why we had to leave her daddy.

I would say my heart broke for her as I watched her sweet little five-year-old self try to understand the pain she was feeling, but mine was already broken. Leaving Liam behind was the last thing I wanted to do. More than anything, I wanted our family to be reunited. I wanted to stay just as much as Anna did, but we had to make a choice. There was a difference in our lifestyles. Where I covered myself with the blood of Jesus and let Him fight a battle against evil that I couldn't win by myself, Liam rejected Jesus was still trying to fight a losing battle with the devil by himself.

No matter how bad things inside of me got during my walk with the demon, Jesus's quiet whispers of love and authority kept me sane enough to take the next step, not hurt anyone or myself, and care for my daughter. Our material needs were provided for, our hearts were protected, and peace was given to us when we needed it. On the other hand, as

Liam continued to curse God and reject his love, I watched his life fall down around him.

After thinking for a moment about my answer to Anna as we drove across the Missouri River in pouring rain, I said to her, "Daddy's heart is sick." This is all I knew to say to her.

When we got back to Michigan, time passed slowly. Most days still felt like torture because my anxiety was so bad, and Anna's behavior showed me that her feelings inside weren't much better than mine. She had been through a lot of traumatic changes for a 5-year-old.

Life was tough for a little while, but we went to church and clung to Jesus. My parents and family took care of us, and eventually, with the help of my grandma, I moved myself, Anna, and our dogs into a little apartment. Before I knew it, I was holding my baby girl, Ellie, in my arms for the first time.

When Ellie was born, the doctor laid her on my chest, and without a cry and with her eyes wide open, she peacefully looked up at me with her deep brown dark eyes. She blinked slowly, looked around carefully, and listened to my voice. Not a peep came from her mouth. It was at that moment that I knew she was a miracle.

The amount of stress I experienced during her pregnancy was more than enough to create more than one health problem for her, yet she was born healthy and peaceful. As she grew older, this peacefulness continued. Just like how God saved me from the demon, her entrance into the world, her health, and her demeaner was a miracle from God.

****

After having a baby, the anxiety I already had from the demon reached a peak and it was no longer manageable. I called my mom one evening asking her for advice and support, and she suggested that I go to the doctor. To be honest, I was way past the point of needing to go to the doctor, and I knew that. Somewhere along the line, I developed a dislike and opinion for medicating mental health issues with medication, and I felt weak for even contemplating it. Although I was good at hiding it, I was at a breaking point. Each day, I would barely make it to the late morning before I burst into tears. Sometimes, I'd turn my head and hide my face as I drove Anna to school in the morning as I cried, and I often stood over the stove and cooked dinner while tears ran down my face. Medication was a last resort I was willing to try, and I was way past the point of needing it.

I started taking medication for the anxiety I experienced after seeking my doctor's help, and the relief I felt was immediate and peaceful. I was able to enjoy life and have present moments with my daughters, and mostly, I could breathe again. Where before it felt like someone was sitting on my chest, with a little bit of adjustment of the dosage, weight was finally lifted off my chest, and I could breathe again.

Slowly, little miracles began to surround my family and cover our lives. When we moved before the baby was born, I looked forward to the future with dread as I was a single mom with no job, no house, no income, debilitating mental health, two children, a car that needed fixed, and a daughter who also needed behavior and trauma intervention, but with time, blessings filled our lives. One by one, blessings from God fell into place at the right time and in the right order. The demon was gone, my mental health improved, we had a place to live, Anna's behavior and wellbeing improved, I found daycare for Ellie, I was offered a job, and Anna and I could both enjoy life again. Over and over again, God answered my prayers, and he gave us things, all kinds of things, tangible and intangible, before I even

asked Him for it.

Chapter 9: A Look Backwards

It wasn't until much later while I was taking Ellie on a run in

a jogging stroller in the brisk Michigan fall weather that I

realized what God had pulled me out of. After having the

interaction with the demon at the apartment in South Carolina

when it strangled me, it was evident to me (most of the time) that I was dealing with evil while I was suffering. It wasn't until I was well out of the pit he pulled me out of and I was thinking back to the times that I sat by myself talking to something that was only heard in my head, arguing with it, yelling at it, feeling it touch me, and having full-blown conversations with it out loud that I realized that what I went through was what society refers to as schizophrenia.

When I spoke to my mom over the phone and Paster Harley before I was baptized, I remember saying to them, *I'm not crazy, I know I'm not schizophrenic, it's the demon from the apartment.*

I said this because from an outside perspective, I had all the qualities of a schizophrenic person. If you open up the DSM-5 (the manual that mental health professionals use for diagnosing mental health conditions), I could place a check mark next to each criterion for schizophrenia. It wasn't until I was finally able to breathe and operate outside of survival mode that I was able to look back and see that schizophrenia was exactly what I was going through and that schizophrenia isn't schizophrenia at all. It's a demon possession and demon oppression.

As this realization came to fruition, it all made sense. I finally understood why the demon, the devil, and all of hell wanted me dead. The battle I'd been through was unusual and unique, and it was all because of what would happen if I survived. The devil understands that Jesus was the only one who could make sense of my experience and deliver me from it, and that is why it tried so hard to separate me from Him. The devil understands Jesus' power, and it didn't want me to survive long enough to get to get to the point of sharing my testimony and releasing his secret. He wanted me to kill myself before I could look back, make sense of my journey, and see the hand of God in my situation. He didn't want me finding out that he lingers behind the scenes of schizophrenia, plucking the strings of people's brains, and playing with them like puppets.

There was a reason my head and my life felt like a warzone, and it's because they were a warzone. It was a fight for life to get to the point of divulging a secret that could save many people in the name of Jesus Christ. At any point in time, Jesus could have rebuked the demon, hell, and all its tricks from my body and mind like I begged Him too, but He chose not to because he saw me on the other side of my journey in the future.

Now, I look back at my life and see exactly why God let me suffer. I see why he didn't take away the demon, its voices, and its terror when I begged Him. If He took the demon out of my life the first time I asked, I wouldn't have made it to the point of hearing voices, feeling the demon's coldness on my skin, and communicating with it. No matter how horrible it felt, the pain and the suffering that I went through was exactly what I needed to look back and see purpose in my testimony. Some things you cannot understand without going through them, and a demon possession is one of them. Through my suffering, while I begged God, day in and day out, for help and pleaded on my knees with tears and snot rolling down my face for him to free me of the demon and all of hell that seemed to be crashing down on my life, He already saw me in the future walking away from my baptism free. He saw me surviving each day to come, getting better, having a healthy baby girl, handling my anxiety in many ways, and writing this book to you. While all I saw at the time was my pain, He saw the millions of people around the world that experience demon possession and call it schizophrenia that are in pain too. If God would have answered my prayer the first time that I asked Him to take the demon out of my life, I would have never been through the process of spiritual resurrection.

I'm not sure what your situation is, and I don't know what keeps you up at night and wakes you up at 3 a.m., but what I do know for sure is that we all have at least one thing in our lives that we would gladly excuse if we had the option. Where I was strangled physically, mentally, and spiritually by a demon, you have your own story and trauma that's occurring in your life and makes you question God's power and love. You wonder why He isn't answering a specific prayer or question, and you can't understand why He is letting you consistently suffer in some way that is unique to you.

Take this from a person that was possessed by a demon while seeking and worshiping God the entire duration of it: if God hasn't answered your prayer yet, it's for a very good reason. A reason that will benefit you and others. If you would have asked me while I was living with the demon if I would have chosen this path for my life, I would have said no. While I was living with the demon and being tormented silently by it day in and day out, there was nothing more I wanted than to get rid of it, but looking back at it now, even with the devastation that it caused in my life, I'm extremely thankful that God chose me and trusted me to go through the things I've been through. I can confidently look back and put the pieces of the puzzle together and watch the full picture come together and answer questions I had before it all happened and during it. On the other side of your suffering is a purpose. If you'll let Him, He will bring you through it for a great purpose.

Now, instead of asking God why He let me suffer so greatly and live with a demon from hell, I now have a better question. How many people will be saved because He kept me alive through the darkness I went through to tell my testimony? How many people will He free from the grips of hell, their lithium medication, and their psychiatric unit because got gave me the privilege of suffering so I could share my testimony to His power and promise?

Part II

Chapter 10: Help

When you go through something traumatic, you can still feel

stuck when you're out of it because your body and mind only

know how to operate in survival mode. Coming to Jesus and

letting him be a part of your life and fight your battles is only

one part to the process (the most important part), but a second and necessary part of the battle is learning a new version of normal and feeling human again.

After I was baptized, it was clear to me that I was saved and no longer trapped by the demon like chains around my wrists, but what debilitated me almost just as much as the prison I was previously in with the demon was the PTSD symptoms and survival mode I was stuck in from my experience. The voices left my mind, and the demon no longer clung to my body, touched my face, or grabbed me with its cold touch. However, I felt debilitated despite its absence. I experienced trauma responses like anxiety and fear so intensely that I felt like nothing was working to make myself feel better. Often, I sat crying, shaking, and out of breath simply trying to calm myself down to do simple tasks. The smallest inconveniences and disruptions would flood my body with adrenaline leaving me feeling heavy and stagnant. There was so much going on in my mind that my body grew physically exhausted from the anxiety I experienced all day long.

I prayed to God for help with this, and at first, he took my discomfort away from me and covered me with him peace. However, after a while of Him showing me that he could and would help me with it, I entered a phase where God wanted me to learn how to calm and soothe myself with his help instead of simply expecting him to wave a magic wand and fix my condition like he pretty much had been doing. He walked me through a process of healing with him.

The following is a short guide for dealing with the aftermath of trauma.

Chapter 11: Don't Talk About It

The first thing I learned about trauma was that reliving it in any way will not help you recover. AT ALL. Talking about it, thinking about it, or recalling anything that you've been through takes time, and if you do it too early, you will send you down a winding path full of PTSD episodes. In fact, I've learned that some instances of trauma are so severe that they may never be able to be talked about by the person who experienced them.

The problem with many mental health professionals who specialize in helping people coping with trauma is that they haven't been through something severe enough themselves to be able to accurately and effectively help other people who have. Everyone deals with some kind of trauma in their life; you can't make it through a lifespan without getting hit by some kind of unfortunate circumstance or treatment, but there are levels and versions of trauma that are more severe than others. The more severe and prolonged the trauma, the more damage it does to your brain, psyche, and body. A person who experienced the divorce of their parents may find it beneficial to talk about their feelings and the events that occurred with a therapist, but someone that has experienced a prolonged and intense period of trauma such as a six-month deployment in a warzone that involved patrolling through enemy territory in the dark at night, bloodshed, and constant anticipation of an enemy encounter will probably not find revisiting their trauma helpful at all.

When the demon was finally removed from my life, I'd experienced so much trauma that talking about it sent me into full-blown episodes of PTSD where I thought I was going to die. Where some trauma can be revisited, some

cannot. The goal isn't to be able to talk about the trauma to

work through it like many mental health professionals want,

the goal is to function normally again. So, as a golden rule,

if you've experienced a level of trauma that is this severe,

don't talk about it. Don't talk about it. Don't talk about it.

Don't talk about it.

Chapter 12: Pray

When you experience trauma symptoms, usually your mind isn't in the right place to form a coherent plan or make a smart decision. Even if you have a trauma safety plan already made for yourself, it's hard to remember what you already know when you're in the middle of an anxiety attack, a panic attack, or you're reliving an instance of trauma.

When I say that the first thing you should do when you start experiencing a trauma response is pray, I don't mean that that praying will serve the purpose of asking God step into the middle of your feelings to simply take them away from you, but for him to give you direction. Your prayer doesn't have to be a long prayer, as this would be difficult if you're truly experiencing symptoms of severe trauma, but simply calling on God with a word or two is all you need

When I experienced PTSD symptoms and I was out of breath, hyperventilating, and crying, all I could make out sometimes was, "Jesus, help." Sometimes, Peter's famous words, "Lord, save me," came to mind, but anything will work. "Jesus, I can't breathe. What do I do?" Often, I prayed, "God, it's happening again," and that's all I could make out.

It sounds stupid and simple, but when you start with God instead of your own toolbox, He will show you what to do or point to the next thing for you to do to cope, calm yourself down, and be functionable .

Now, if you ask God for help, expect Him to respond. Often, God speaks to us through thoughts (not all the time; we have some awful thoughts too), so if you get a thought in response to your cry for help and you even think it might be

God, go with it.

When I ask God for help when I find myself in this

debilitating condition, in the middle of my mind that spinning

like a tornado in anxiety and panic, He comes across to me

as a thought that says, *Go for a walk.* Or sometimes it's an

answer as simple as *gym* or *draw.* Sometimes, he points me

to other steps we will talk about after this chapter, and He

will answer with *list.* No matter what the answer is or what

He will tell you to do, one this is for sure is that He will

answer you. He will give you the help you need, even if you

don't like the answer.

Chapter 13: Change The Channel

There are many grounding techniques that therapists teach people who have been through trauma, but unfortunately, they are only helpful if you are able to focus on them and fully engage in them. For example, sometimes, people are taught to list objects by color in their surroundings or name items according to their senses. This can be helpful, but again, if you're experiencing a true trauma episode, I can almost guarantee that these types of exercises are not going to work for their intended purpose. So, instead of making lists that participate in these grounding exercises, make a list of things that you like to do. Make a list of things that are fun for you, that include your hobbies, and disconnect you from the world around you.

The purpose of this is to give you a reference. If you've ever been to a hotel and turned on the TV, it helps to have a channel guide to see what number each channel is on. The list you create for yourself will act like a reference to you in a time of need to help you change the channel that your mind is operating on. Instead of trying to function in survival mode, engaging in one of the activities on your list will automatically switch your brain into relaxation mode where you can think and live freely.

The things I made on my list include activities such as going for a walk or run, drawing or painting, lifting weights, playing with my daughters, playing with my dogs, cleaning my house, doing laundry, going to the beach, playing my ukulele, and baking. Often when I start this process with praying to God for help, he points me to my list where I can engage in something on it that switches the mode I'm operating in and fixes my anxiety or panic.

Your list is only helpful if it's available to you. Be creative where you keep it available for yourself and keep the list in places like the note app on your phone, a list that you keep in your car, or on a paper that hangs above your sink in your bathroom. Keep it in places where it's easy access or where you think you might need it.

Chapter 14: Tell The Truth

Like listing activities, make a list of things that you know are true and will help you while you experience an episode of PTSD or anxiety. List your affirmations about yourself and about Jesus. For example, things I tell myself are:

1. I am okay.

2. It's alright.

3. Nothing's going to hurt me.

4. This isn't real.

5. God's in charge.

6. God's got my back.

7. God is not against me.

8. God loves me.

9. God wants me to win.

10. God wants me to succeed.

11. God knows what I need more than I do.

12. No isn't no, it's direction.

13. I am enough for where God has put me.

14. I feel worried, but I am okay.

15. If the devil could have killed me, he would have already.

Make a list of anything that might help you that you know to be true (biblical and nonbiblical). Put these in places where they are available to you or where you may need them just like the other list. Keep them in your pocket, write something on your hand, hang a sticky note up, or make them the background on your phone. You put them where you need them.

Chater 15: Reflect

The last thing to do, which I've intentionally put last, is

reflect. I don't mean reflect on your trauma or the event that

caused it, I mean reflect back on what made you feel the way

you felt during your episode of PTSD or during the time you

experience PTSD symptoms that made you need to pray and

use your lists. This is important because if you can do this,

you can pinpoint what caused this reaction, prepare for it in

the future, and, maybe, even prevent it in the future.

I'm sure you've heard the term trigger before, and

essentially what you need to do is identify your triggers.

Once you've calmed down and are in a state of relaxation, if

you can, think back to your surroundings or the situation that

occurred around you when you started feeling upset. Ask

yourself the question, "What happened that made me feel that

way?" Sometimes the trigger will be blatantly obvious to

you, sometimes it won't. If you can't identify it, ask God.

"God, what made me feel that way?" Involving God always

helps.

In the past when I reflected, I noticed that the things

that were causing my anxiety and PTSD symptoms were

things that occurred around me in the present that had

previously been associated with meanings that the demon

spoke to me. When I looked back on my anxiety attacks and

when they started, I noticed that they occurred after I came in

contact with certain objects, songs, people, smells, or tastes

that were associated with my trauma in any way. One

example is when my dog had a bathroom accident inside.

Understanding that my dog having an accident in the house

was a trigger for me, I was able to prepare and combat my anxiety before it came on or before it became a full-blown anxiety attack or an episode of PTSD where I thought I was back in the depths of hell.

Instead of going down the road of panicking, hyperventilating, crying, and feeling like I was having a heart attack and dying when my dog used the bathroom inside, I was able to take my phone out, look at my lists, tell myself truths and engage in an activity that would channel me out of panic and survival.

Depending on how much trauma you have been through, you may have to do this over and over and over again to pinpoint all the triggers you have, but if you can, it

will be worth it. At some point, I identified certain times of

the day, objects, and other things in my day as triggers, so I

preplanned for them and hung sticky note reminders and

changed my daily routine up as I needed to avoid or mitigate

the effects of my triggers as much as possible.

Chapter 16: Altered

At some point on my journey of healing, I was very thankful because I felt somewhat normal again. My days slowly grew easier, and I was able to enjoy life more and more and accomplish daily tasks easier. One thing I noticed, though, was that I was only able to help myself so much. I was managing triggers effectively, avoiding as many detrimental emotions as possible, and able to move forward with life little by little.

Where things that were once triggers for me seemed to trigger me less and less as time continued, I noticed that if anything bad happened in my life, it took me out for days. Things that would have once been little bumps in the road felt like roadblocks that wouldn't be gotten over, and I was easily filled and flooded with sadness, fear, and exhaustion. Little things like a car beeping its horn at me on the road or dropping my coffee on the ground made me so upset that I'd cry for an hour, and it ruined my mood for a long time.

Rather than simply feeling irritated by little hiccups in my day, I felt them deep down and they were whole-body encompassing debilitating events.

Eventually, I had to come to terms with the fact that my brain's chemical makeup and ability to function was changed by my trauma. I wasn't as naturally resilient as I once was before it occurred. My neural pathways were changed, and my nervous system and the way my body processes the different chemicals that are involved in experiencing pain were no longer the same. I needed help that was beyond my behavior change. I needed biological change: medicine.

I've always been against taking medication for mental health reasons, but by experience, I had to accept the fact that I was no longer the same person I was before the trauma. My brain wasn't working the same anymore, and I needed medical help. I began taking an SSRI, Lexapro, and for the first time in a long time, I felt normal again. No longer did I just burst out in tears because of trivial events that I should have been able to just step over, and I could sit down with my daughters and enjoy time with them. I felt brand new.

At some point, when we experience enough trauma, our brains aren't the same anymore, and even with behavioral intervention, you cannot achieve a normal level of functioning. If this is you, maybe it's time to talk to your doctor about medication. I was once strictly against medicating for mental health, but if you're like me, you may find that medication is a miracle in disguise just waiting for you to set your ego and personal opinions aside.

Conclusion

One thing that I've learned from my experience living with

the demon and recovering from it is that what I thought was

impossible can be possible with the help of God. There were

many times that I stood frozen in time with a situation in front

of me that felt impossible and looked the size of Mount

Everest. There were things that God brought me through and out of that I thought I'd be stuck in for forever. I thought the demon would kill me, and I thought I'd be possessed for the rest of my life. Once it was gone, I thought I wouldn't ever feel normal again, and I never imagined that I would be able to write about my experience coherently.

No matter what you're going through, recovering from, or where you've been, God will see you through and bring you out if you let Him. He will give you purpose, use your trauma, mistakes, and everything that's happened in your life to fulfill a purpose that will be better than anything you could have imagined. Whatever you do, wherever you

are, and however, you feel, look to God and just keep going.

Part III

Change the Channel
My list of channels (relaxation activities)

1.

2.

3.

4.

5.

6.

7.

8.

9.

My Truths
I am okay. I am loved. God's got my back. He's got this.

1.

2.

3.

4.

5.

6.

7.

8.

My Triggers

1.

2.

3.

4.

5.

6.

7.

8.

9.

10.

Notes:

Doodles: